I0180273

ISBN 1-84481-970-1

This ebook edition published 2008

The Ultimate Guide to the Perfect Relationship

Published by New Line Publishing, 118 Gatley Road, Cheadle, Cheshire, SK8 4AD, UK.

Find us on the World Wide Web at: www.ultimateguidetotheperfectrelationship.com
This eBook is made available at: www.ultimateguidetotheperfectrelationship.com

Editing, cover and interior design by WebDirectStudio
www.webdirectstudio.com (website)
info@webdirectstudio.com (email)

The Ultimate Guide to the Perfect Relationship

Alisa Miller

NewLine
Publishing

"…This is something we take for granted and something we expect to be there by default. The thing is that every relationship takes work in order to work for both of you and then keep on working for a long time".

Alisa Miller

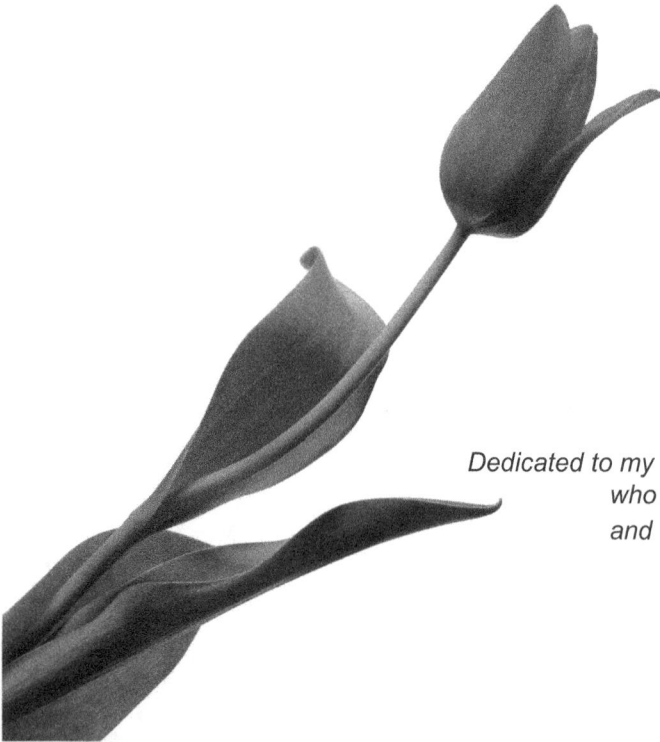

Dedicated to my beloved husband David who was there to inspire me and help me write this book.

Table of Contents

Introduction

A relationship between two people is always complicated no matter how well you match. It gets to be even more complicated if you don't match at all. Love is a wonderful feeling but it's very sensitive just like a flower and it needs a lot of care in order to keep on blooming. How often do you hear stories about two people living together for a long time and being madly in love till the very end? And how often do you hear divorce stories and stories of broken families? For some reason people think that once they get married or have at least 4 years of joint life together they will be loved and cared for by their partner no matter what for the rest of their days.

But why? People change, their feelings change and the little lovely sparkling light you were treasuring so deep goes from your lives forever.

But it doesn't have to be this way! You can make your love last forever. Well at least for as long as you care about your love lasting. If you really care about your partner and about your relationship this little light of happiness, however soppy this may sound, will never leave your sight.

Just imagine: you can be in love forever, you can enjoy the company of your partner all your life day after day and each day can feel special because you are with your partner. Isn't this happiness?

Imagine if you have all the money in the world, all the things you ever wanted, all the things you ever wanted to achieve – achieved but no one to share all that with? Things and titles only make sense if you are able to share them with someone because all the money in the world can never buy you true happiness. And lonely people, people with dead hearts can never be really happy though they could have anything they want in the world.

Being loved and giving love back is above everything else you can possibly imagine and it's worth fighting for. Don't make the same mistakes others made! This book will help you to understand your partner better, improve your relationship and give you the knowledge which will help you to avoid many traps on your way to happiness. It will bring harmony into your hearts. You will enjoy your partner and love each other for the rest of your life!

I have, on purpose, avoided putting in case studies, writing complicated methodologies, loading you down with theories and research studies. The truth is that each relationship is different and we are each different in it and there is no magic formula. If you really want some tech stuff try my website (www.ultimateguidetotheperfectrelationship.com) where I routinely use research material to cover relevant aspects of dating and relationships, or try reading one of the more tech-heavy books on the market.

This book is a guide. As a guide it works best if you think about it, internalise its seemingly simple message and make it your own and use it to guide you in getting the relationship you want.

I am giving you the Ultimate Guide to the Perfect Relationship you deserve.

Alisa Miller

Before you start reading...

This book has been written for you to analyze and understand your relationship with your partner no matter at what stage it is at the moment. It doesn't matter if you have been married for 20 years or you are just moving in together, if you have kids or other commitments. This book will help you to understand how your relationship should work and it will help you to make it work no matter how things are at the moment.

Before you start reading you should be committed to helping your relationship, to make it better and make it work. Do not be focused on trying to find faults and mistakes you or your partner made or are still making. This information is for both of you to make your mutual future brighter and way more enjoyable for as long as you both want it.

Remember this is not about finding who is guilty and who is making things difficult. Whatever happened before has happened and there is no turning time back. What you should be concentrating on is the future of your relationship.

Communication is the key

Getting to know each other for real

You can spend years and years living with someone and never know the person you are living with. It happens quite often as these days people have separate lives: they go to work, to the gym, meet their friends, have hobbies on their own - and when the time to go to bed comes – they meet with their partner for the first time in a whole day only so they can say "Good night".

You can carry on like that a whole lifetime but you can hardly enjoy it. People get bored and have affairs trying to find a way out... and it's only because they didn't spend a little bit more time with their partner to get to know each other better and simply talk. Talk is what most couples don't do from the moment they realize they are in a long-term relationship.

Why? The "love dance" is exciting and spontaneous in the beginning when you are fighting for your partner's heart and it's a challenge. But once you fought and won you feel that there is no point in making an effort anymore. Well not as much, let's say.

But actually getting somebody to like you and getting somebody to start living with you is only the beginning of your journey for happiness and no one knows how far you will go if you let your relationship develop on its own. It may end there and then or it may end 20 years later when both of you will eventually realise that it's not working. That's why it's important that you get to know each other before it is already too late for that.

Information

Do you know what your partner's favourite colour is? Do you know what he or she likes doing most of all? Do you know what is his or her the worst nightmare? What your partner's dreams are about? All these are just the obvious questions the answer to which you should know on the third day of dating. In a long-term relationship we stop thinking about the questions and we start relying on our own ideas on what our partner likes and what they do not. And this is the wrong approach to take. People change and their point of view changes through the years (days, months), and their taste certainly changes as well.

So no matter how many times you ask the same question you can get a different answer each time. It's absolutely normal and it is part of being human: developing and analysing the world around us, making judgments and having opinions. So don't be afraid to ask the same thing again as it can help you to avoid a lot of problems in the future. It's better to re-ask something than to rely on the old information and start getting it wrong.

Small talk

Getting to know each other is a long-term goal and yes this goal has no ending. It's a constant process and it is a lot of fun.

Being able to talk about different things and having "small talks" every so often is part of being together and enjoying each other. We lose these small talks from our every day life because they don't seem to be very important. But they are. Talking, discussing, arguing and having a laugh together every day of your joint life is part of the natural bonding upon which strong and happy relationships are built.

But for that you always need to have a subject. It may sound odd but it's not really, it's something you will do naturally once you get a grip. Follow me.

Here are a few ideas...

Get into the habit of reading the newspaper or watching the news together in the morning so that you can talk about it afterwards. This becomes part of your shared culture together where each informs the other's point of view of the world and its workings.

Read the same books. If your partner is reading about gardening you should read sometime the same book as well. It will not just give you something to talk about but it will also help you to understand your partner's behaviour at times (like placing strange plates with seeds on the window sill). At least you will know what's going on in your partner's head and where did he or she get an idea from (that his/her brain is OK, they have not been abducted by aliens after all).

Watch movies together. Get into the habit of choosing movies on a TV guide together during the week and watch them together. It's not just something to talk about it's also your time spent

in each other's company away from every day life's problems.

Go window shopping after the shops are shut. It's cost-effective and helps you to find out what your partner likes and what they do not. When your partner gives you an opinion about something don't just take it as a fact, always give your own opinion back and talk about it. At the end of the conversation you both can have a different point of view about the subject. Make sure that by giving your own opinion you are not being hard and you are not rejecting the opinion of your partner suppressing his or her point of view. Make sure that when you give your opinion and it's opposite to your partner's it sounds soft rather than confrontational. For example: "Really? It's really cool. I am not sure 100% about it, but it's cool".

Start hobbies together. But before you start anything talk about it and make sure both of you are interested. Otherwise you will end up being upset when your partner "is not trying hard enough".

Play together. It can be anything you like from chess to PlayStation. This kind of activity creates in-jokes and your own secret language which is in the every couple 'must have' list.

It's also important that you talk about your relationship and the way it is heading; that you both know what to expect. It's important that you plan your future together and can actually see it clearly.

Being together is like a full-time job where you are not just responsible for yourself, but you also have to think about the other person's needs and feelings. So it is important you know about these needs and you always know how your partner feels as well as letting him or her know about your own needs and feelings.

Communication is the key.

Meaningless things

and how not to fall into the trap of "we have nothing to talk about"

When people meet and fall in love they usually talk non-stop about anything but once they start living together or meeting each other very often for some time all they talk about is things they have to do and what happened to other people. All the things which have no particular meaning but which are there just to fill the space between drinks.

So many times I have seen couples who don't talk at all. Well they talk about things they need to get for the house, where their kids will go after school, about things at work and other people's lives. But they stop talking about their dreams, about their interests and certainly they avoid being in each other's company just for the sake of each other's company. After a while each of the partners starts having a separate life and what happens then is that in yoru relationship you become just two people living under the same roof rather than two people sharing a common journey through life.

Every day, every month, every year you can discover your partner again and again!

People change all the time, they have new interests, they have new points of view, and new experiences they may want to share. It's always important to talk about everything, tell each other how you spent a day if you spent it separately or discuss it and exchange opinions if you spent it together. This is an important aspect of the sharing process. It is part of your common

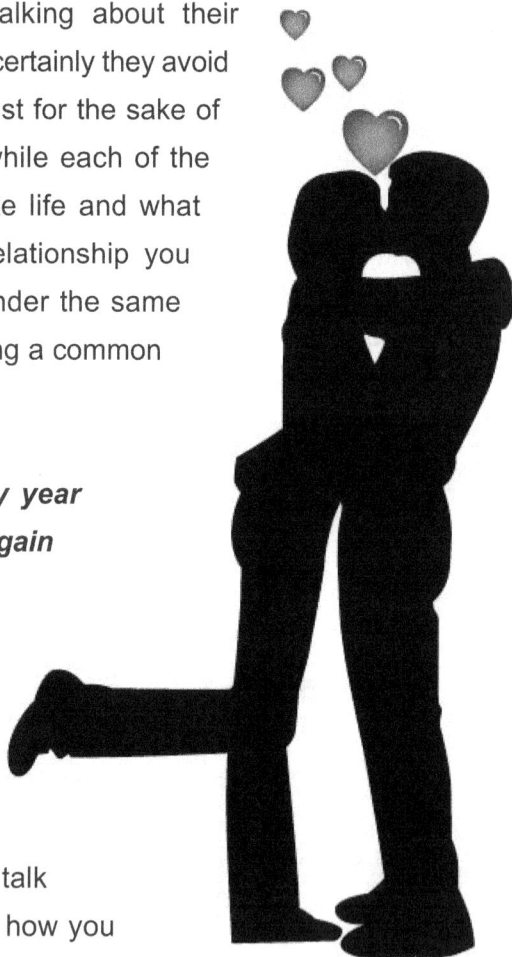

cultural background as a couple.

If one of you has a hobby the other one needs to experience it too. If you're excited about something you absolutely need to share it and the first person in line is your partner.

It can be anything from hobby crafts to martial arts but you need to try it yourself to understand why your beloved likes it. And don't you ever tell him or her that the hobby they have chosen is silly and they need to give it up. No matter what they enjoy doing your responsibility is to support them and try to understand it. You have chosen this person to share your life with so this is part of that sharing and not just the sharing of the living space you cohabit.

Start new hobbies together and don't be afraid to start silly things as you both will enjoy them anyway and if it will not work out you still will have a great time failing.

19

Plus you will have the great benefit of doing new things together which makes them so much less scary.

What is important is that you do things together.

Make it a rule to go for a walk during the week with your partner. You can go to the park, to the café (but not a noisy one where you can't hear each other talk); you can go anywhere where you feel comfortable and you are able to relax and be yourself. This is a time for you and your partner only; there can't be any discussion of work or friends, as this is the time of you to share your feelings, hopes and dreams. After all you are together because you like each other as a couple not because you have friends in common.

List of hobbies you can start together

Photography. You can start taking shots on a particular subject or with no subject whatsoever. It will help you to see the world through each other's eyes and understand each other better.

Learning languages together: you can practise together at home, learn new words and use them every so often in everyday life. It not just helps you to develop your skills and knowledge but it helps the two of you to find a "common language" while learning.

Wine and/or chocolate tasting – can always be a lot of fun; you can even join a night school together. After all you two could even become experts in wine and chocolate and use that knowledge to money from it. And if you fail, well, you still had a sweet time learning about it all!

Cooking courses. Imagine how much easier it can become when it comes to cooking in your life when you both actually understand what you need to do and why! You can read cookery books and/or watch TV programs together. You can invent your own recipe and call it "Kate and Mike's secret recipe" and you can have fun messing about in the kitchen.

Scrapbooking. Nobody remembers how awkward it was taking a shot of you two frozen with Champagne glasses waiting for the flash to go off but everybody loves looking at the pictures afterwards. You can organize your photographs and make scrapbooks of your own, unleashing your creativity! Imagine having something you both can put your souls into and being able to look and touch it every so often. Priceless.

Collecting. You can start a collection together. You can collect pretty much anything from antique books and weapons to teddy bears and whatever both of you are interested in. The thing, always is that you share and in sharing you discover more of each other.

Start an eBay shop. Have you ever thought about it? And yet you can make money from something you created together. Find a product, get inspired and have fun!

Movie making. Have you got a video camera? Why not start making home videos you can edit afterwards where a birthday party suddenly turns into a horror movie for example. Or you can make real movies where you can be the whole movie crew writing, acting and editing.

Start a garden together. It doesn't matter if you have a lot of space in your garden or you hardly have any space in the kitchen corner plans and flowers can fit in house. Creating a small garden is not just a perfect way to spend time together but it's also a very cost effective way to cheer up your living space. Sit down together and go through the garden catalogues, choose flowers together and think on the design. It doesn't have to be a one-evening project (after all it's not cheap to get everything at once) but it can be a long-term one where you add elements to your garden bit by bit. Go to the garden centre together and get inspired. In most garden centres you can find a coffee place where you can spend some time discussing your ideas.

T I P !   Choose a plant and buy the seeds to grow it. Read up online or get a book from the library on this particular plant. Make this plant your own Flower of Love. Look after it together, see it grow and bloom.

Dancing. It's a good skill to have and it's very enjoyable. You and your partner can both join a dancing class or start learning some moves using self-teaching DVDs. You can also find a lot of lessons online. Dancing is something you can practise together. There is an elemental air of excitement in it and it allows you to create a special bond as you learn to dance.

Join a martial arts club together. It's not just about self-defence but also about philosophy and finding your place in this life. Make sure you choose your club very carefully and talk with the teacher before you join. You may also consider joining a yoga class. Or you can do yoga at home using manuals or a DVD.

Questionnaire
To get to know each other better

1) If you could become a super hero who would you be?

2) Are You a Lark, an Owl, or a Hummingbird?

3) Do you like your eggs fried both sides, boiled or in an omelette?

4) Do you like animals? Have you had pets when you were a kid and what were their names?

5) What is your favourite drink? Do you like coffee or tea?

6) What luxury item would you take on a desert island?

7) If you could be successful at any job in the world, what would that job be?

8) Describe your perfect Sunday morning?

9) If you could be someone else for a day, who would it be?

10) If you met the right person, how many children would you have?

11) What was the last book you read? Did you enjoy it?

12) What is the craziest thing you've done lately?

13) What's your favourite colour?

14) What's your favourite chocolate bar?

15) When they make the movie about your life, which actor should portray you?

16) What's the next country you want to visit?

17) Describe a perfect romantic evening.

18) How old were you when you went on your first date? Who was

it with?   Where did you go and what did you do?

19)   Do you like to cook? What's your best meal?

20)   What do you do in your free time that you're absolutely passionate about? Something you could lose yourself in for hours?

21)   What's the longest you've gone without sleep?

22)   What's the habit you're most proud about breaking?

23)   What's your favourite Website?

24)   What do you order when you eat Chinese food?

25)   What costume would you wear at the dress-up party?

26)   Are you afraid of heights?

27)   Have you ever taken dance lessons?

28)   What's your favourite breakfast food?

29)   What's your favourite computer game?

30)   What does your dream house look like?

31)   What's your favourite item of clothing?

32)   Do you have any birthmarks? If so, where?

33)   What is your most embarrassing moment?

34)   Describe a perfect sandwich.

35)   Do you sing in the shower?

36)   What's your favourite fruit pie?

37)   Do you believe in ghosts?

38)   Do you like cartoons? What's your favourite cartoon? Cartoon character?

39)   What do you do when you are feeling very sad or depressed?

40)   What was your favourite childhood toy?

41)   What's your favourite flavour ice-cream?

42)   Which sport do you like?

43)   What super-power would you most like to have, and why?

44)   Do you like flowers? What's your favourite flower?

45)   Are you allergic to anything? Fur, nuts, specific medicine?

46)   How tall are you?

47)   Do you believe in karma? Soul mates? Destiny?

48)   What are the two most sensitive parts of your body?

49)   What kind of clothing do you find sexy?

50)   How would you describe "being in love"?

Spending time together and apart

The time you spend together is very-very special. And it's not just when you are together in one room, but it's when you are truly together, holding each other's hand, looking into each other's eyes, talking and enjoying every minute. Because these things are so obvious people manage to ignore them and never actually experience them.

When was the last time you and your partner were sitting together in one room where there is no TV playing and with no friends about? When was the last time you went for a walk in the park – just you and your partner?

The time you spend in each other's company is very important for both of you. And you need to find time for each other no matter how busy you are.

Far too often we use work as an easy excuse to avoid seeing each other. The moment you realise that this is not an acceptable way to behave in a relationship with someone you love you should stop using it.

JUST THINK! what does it matter if you will earn a lot of money and have a great career when there is no one to share it with?

It's very easy to stop treasuring each other once you start living together. You stop paying too much attention to what each of you is doing and feeling because you just get too busy dealing with everyday tasks and problems. This is when fault lines which have began to develop in yoru relationship can become true rifts and drive you apart.

Few ideas

on how to spend time together and enjoy it

TAKE A DAY OFF
AND GO ON A PICNIC

Take a blanket, some wine and sandwiches and off you go. Spend the whole day together out once in a while, play truant from your responsibilities. Talk and enjoy each other's company. Don't forget that this is what you are there for and it doesn't matter if one of you forgot something at home, the weather sucks or there are millions of unresolved problems which are waiting for you back at home. It's your time and it's just for the two of you.

GO TO THE ZOO TOGETHER

Well, just assigning your family members to monkeys and lizards or other animals can be a lot of fun but also the fact that you are there to experience something together means a lot. There is a game you can also play there: you need to find a quality of the animal you think your partner has and then your partner has to do the same for you so you will take turns. You can't repeat the same animals during the game. For example: "You are brave like a lion", "You are beautiful like a snow butterfly", "You are cheeky like a squirrel". The point is it's yoru time to be together in a way that's uniquly your own. Enjoy it!

GO TO THE THEATRE OR MUSEUM

It's always interesting to see the way your partner sees things and it's a perfect opportunity to share your thoughts and ideas.

Find out what both of you would like to see and go ahead. You must remember this is never a waste of time and it's very important that you do all these things because this is when the two of you are really bonding. You need to get away from the reality of everyday life and spend some time exploring each other's personalities. This is your private, shared space which no one else is privy too.

GO TO THE CINEMA

Leave your friends & family at home and go together just the two of you. Because these two experiences are totally different – when you are going with friends you are going to be connecting to every member of the group and you will never concentrate on your partner. When you are going alone with your loved one it's a special time when you become two best allies going through the adventure on the screen.

GO SKATING

(or ice-skating if possible)
and have some real fun!

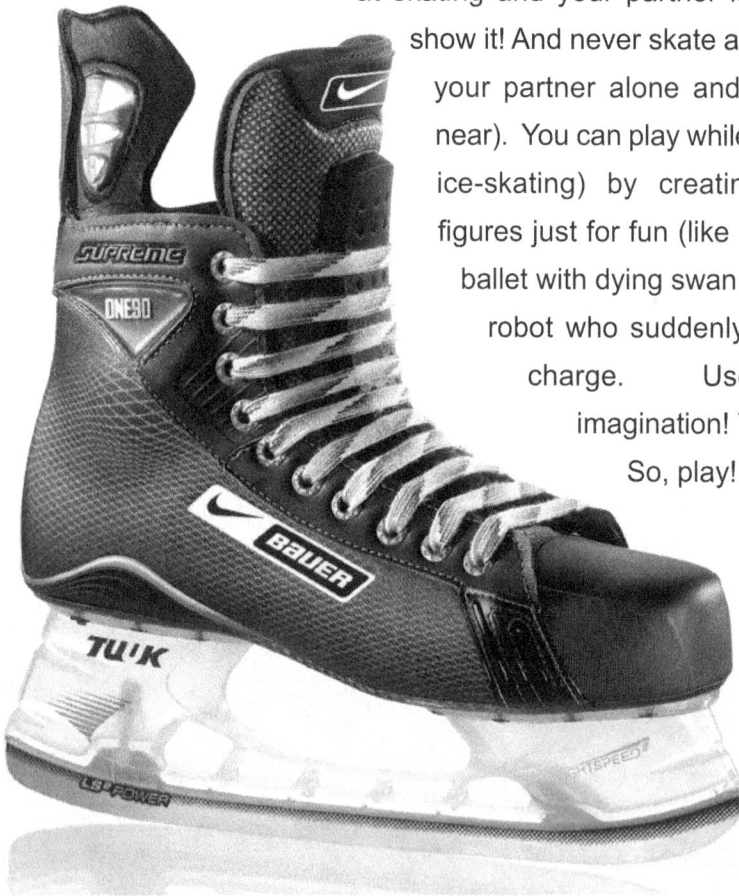

There is nothing as exciting as falling and getting bruises when your partner is by your side. Race each other (but not for real, this is not a competition! If you are good at skating and your partner is not never show it! And never skate away leaving your partner alone and be always near). You can play while skating (or ice-skating) by creating different figures just for fun (like doing some ballet with dying swan poses) or a robot who suddenly ran out of charge. Use your imagination! This is play. So, play!

GO ON A CITY-WALK

It's a good opportunity to find out what's going on in your area and enjoy each other's company at the same time. Make a little adventure and investigate all the little corners of your city, exchange memories and opinions. You can find some places you both like and make them your own, like a favourite café or a little corner somewhere in the park.

GO WINDOW-SHOPPING

You don't have to buy anything but you can discuss things around you. That way you will always know what your partner thinks about particular things and it also makes it easier to choose Christmas and birthday gifts. Never mind it can be a lot of fun for both of you.

Remember the difference between men and women, acknowledgment and action – men never just say something because they just just say it, they need an action to follow the words and women just say things because they share their thoughts. So if a woman says she likes something it doesn't necessarily mean she wants it and wants it now. It may sound like a small thing but many an argument has started because of it.

GO ON A DATE

Amazingly a lot of people stop actually dating each other once they become a couple. But why stop? You should always have these special moments in your life when you go through the process of charming each other again and again? You can go to a restaurant together or you can stay at home but what really matters is you understand and prepare yourself not just for an ordinary dinner but a date, complete with candle light and dressing up for the occasion.

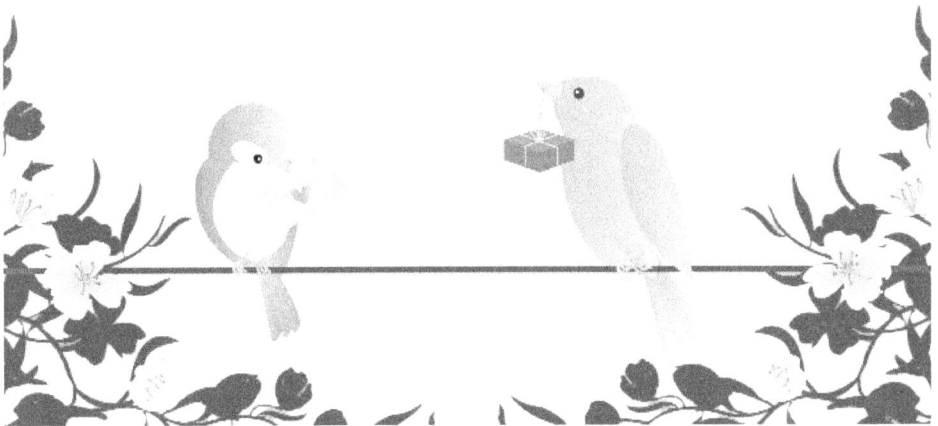

GO SWIMMING

Have you ever tried swimming with fins? Well it's a lot of fun for both of you as when you are swimming with fins you don't get as tired as fast so you can enjoy chasing each other and playing games in the water. A lot of swimming pools have water towers and you can always find some sea sports by the sea side. Frolic in the water. It's easy, it's fun and it's carefree.

STAY AT HOME MOVIE WATCHING

You can always rent a DVD and watch it together at home! Make your own pop corn and/or order a pizza, go through the movies you would like to watch together and spend all evening in each other's arms.

TIP! You can make your own pizza beforehand working with your partner to choose ingredients you both like the most. If you can't decide then make it half and half. Be creative and have fun!

PLAY TOGETHER

You can play together at home like a game of chess or monopoly or you can go out and play some air hockey or bowling. It doesn't matter what it is. What's most important is it will be just the two of you spending time together.

When you are alone it's time to think and analyze your feelings. Are you missing your partner? Are you feeling better when your partner is gone? It's important that you always stay aware of your own feelings and can spot a doubt before it's too late.

Sometimes you may be too much all over your partner and there is not enough breathing space for two of you so when it comes to leaving each other you feel much better finally staying alone.

But it is wrong and it shouldn't be that way.

So it is important that you don't just spend much time together but you spend some time doing your own thing and letting your partner have some personal time as well. But try not to overdo one or the other. There has to be a balance when it comes to spending time together and spending time apart. You can stay in the same room for hours and you will be pretty much apart doing your own thing and again you can be doing something together where you very much connect with each other.

T I P ! If you are away from your partner for a long time when coming back bring something nice to surprise him (or her) with a little gesture. It can be a flower, or a sweet, or something unexpected like singing under a window or anything else you may think of. A little bit of romance is always good for the relationship.

Mirror, Mirror...

You will be surprised to hear (or maybe you have heard about it before) if two people mirror each other they connect. It's a neurolinguistic programming (NLP) technique that can be practised but really it's also an absolutely natural way of connecting with another person on a subconscious level. You can do it consciously as well.

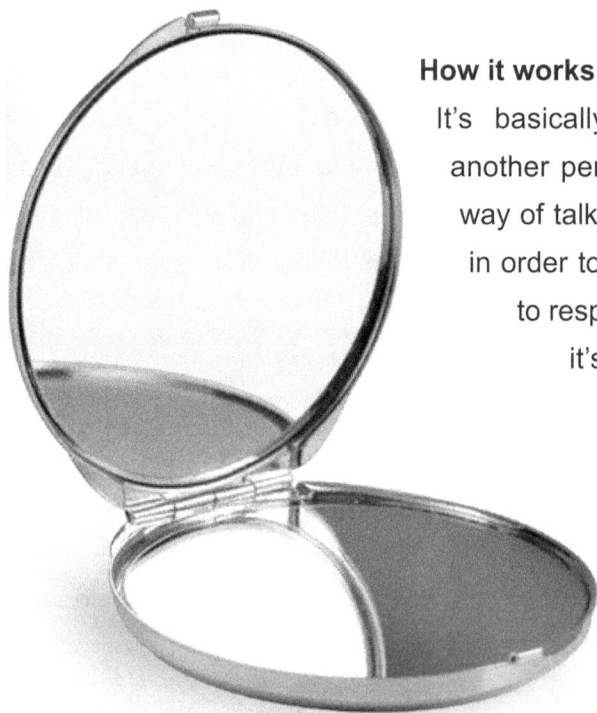

How it works

It's basically a way of copying another person's actions and the way of talking, poses and mimics in order to make another person to respond positively. It's why it's called the mirror effect.

How do you benefit?

You connect. It's that simple. You may do it naturally you may not but the result is the same. You start forcing yourself to act like the other person, inherit the habits and expressions. You'll be surprised but the other person will do the same with you. It will be a fair exchange.

How do you apply it to your relationship?

Copy everything your partner does but not in an obvious artificial way. Use the same gestures while talking as your partner does, take the same poses. Copy the look and the way your partner reacts to particular things. But make it natural and never overdo it otherwise it will have the opposite effect.

T I P ! Do what your partner does during the meal. If you partner drinks you drink as well. If your partner has some salad you have some as well. It's not just good for keeping a conversation going (you can't talk with your mouth full!) but it also helps you to connect.

Differences

AGE DIFFERENCE

Age difference doesn't matter if you truly want things to work for both of you. It doesn't matter who says what and what they write in "clever books" and glossy magazines. If it's real and if it is love the age difference will never matter.

It can be 5 years or 30 between you and your partner your relationship will work and will work around it.

Problems

As it happens there are certain problems when it comes to couples with a big age difference as they belong to different age groups and have different education and social skills as well as a different shared pop-cultural background. Also one of the partners will be more experienced and it can cause problems on practical aspects and judgments when it comes to it.

Solutions

The solution is always to talk and understand what causes each problem. When it comes to experience on information and passed years then it's easy and all you need to do is to catch up! These days you can get all the information online or rent any DVD needed when it comes to music, video and culture.

CULTURAL DIFFERENCE

Problems

It can cause a lot of problems if you come from different cultures and you are not very familiar with each other's country and cultural customs. You will have problems over small and silly things simply because you come from different backgrounds and had different upbringing. So...

You never let things just go and see what happens. If you feel for each other you always make sure your relationship is protected against silliness and lack of information which leads to arguments and misunderstandings.

Solutions

If it is possible you should visit the other partner's country and experience some of the customs, see it and feel its culture and try to understand it.

Ask your partner about his (or her) country when you have a chance or when you are in the middle of something (e.g. "And how do you do it in your country?")

Do your research and find out everything you can about your partner's culture (you can do it online, you can go to the library, you can rent a DVD)

Introduce your own culture to your partner and explain how things are around here (surprisingly some people think its something other people just figure out themselves as time passes).

Finances

Living together and sharing one life means having a common budget where both of you put everything you earn. No exceptions. If you think you can have a very good relationship and passionate love between each other but keep your finances separate you are wrong because it will never work very well for either of you.

Keeping your finances a secret will create all sort of problems the main of which (and the base for all the rest really) is mistrust. If you don't know who earns what and where the money goes you've got serious problems with judgment and expectations as well.

But having a common budget is not an easy task either and you have to be very careful how well you control the money flow. And there is always a cash flow you need to understand.

So first of all you sit down and write things down so you both know how much each of your earns and how much you need to pay monthly for the rent (mortgage), electricity, tax, monthly subscriptions (even small ones like a newspaper subscription), food and medical bills on average.

Make a list and discuss it. It also helps a great deal when you actually know the numbers when it comes to saving and managing your budget and deciding where you can save and where you can spend more than usual.

Whatever you buy has a price. If it comes from your common budget you should let your partner know about the amount spent. There is a tendency here to feel restricted or under someone else' control. Much of this comes from how this 'giving account to someone' thing is done. Work at it like two adults who really love each other and there should be no issue.

What if it's too early to have the same bank account?

If it's still early days and you both are not ready to put all your eggs in one bank account basket then you still need to talk and write things down on the money subject and discuss who is paying for what. It helps you to avoid problems on money mismanagement and false expectations.

The space

Living together and enjoying it

Both of you need to know where things are and how things work. If you move something you always have to tell the other person where the thing is now and where it can be found. Make sure that things always go where they supposed to and keep the house organized. It's OK to have chaos in your living space when you are living on your own but when you are sharing your life with someone else you need to make it as easy as possible for both of you to accept things. So many arguments can be avoided if you keep the house clean, welcoming and person friendly.

The best way to keep organized is to create an interactive plan of the flat/house with the movable objects in it.

T I P ! You can surprise each other with new items and secret treasures like on a pirate map – just draw a cross with the words "Dig here".

A small house is a problem because you can't get away from each other and you will begin to get annoyed over small things just because there is no privacy. But a big house on the other hand holds an even bigger problem

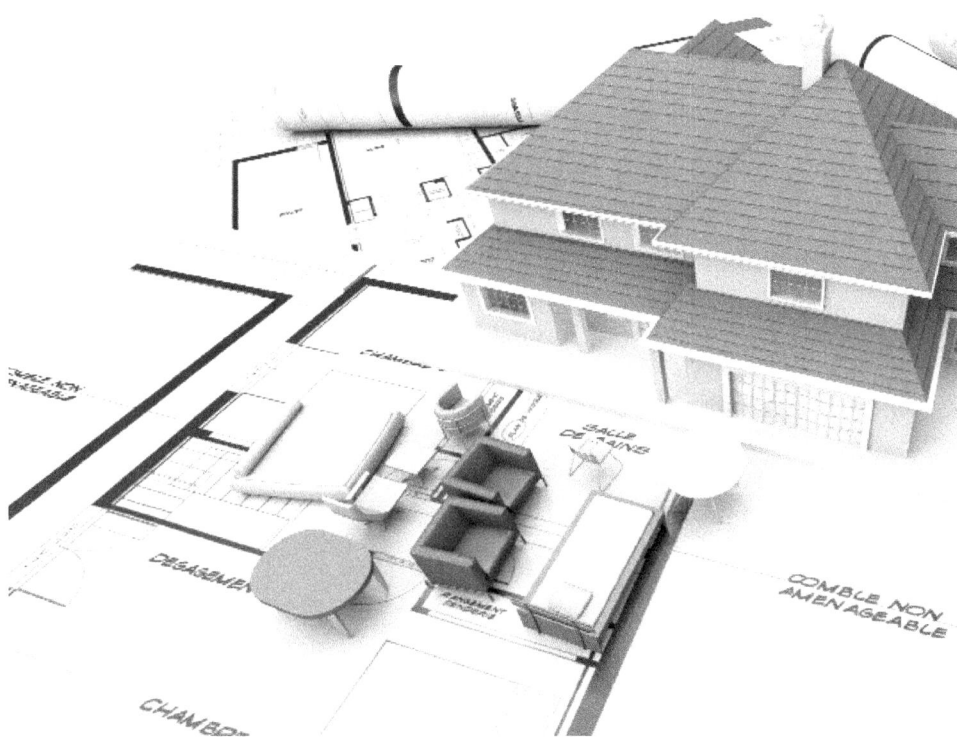

because it gives you ideal conditions for escaping each other. In both cases the only option in order to make things work for both of you is to talk, make compromises and agree on every little detail of your life. It may sound complicated but it can be a lot of fun in the end and it's really worth it.

Buying for the house and receiving gifts from friends and relatives

Always make sure that you both like something you are just about to buy

for the house or something you just received as a gift from your family or friends. Sometimes small things can annoy the hell out of you and you have to be able to tell it to your partner straight away. Your living space belongs to both of you and it is important that you both like the way it looks and feels. Only then can you really call it home.

Your home and your personality

Your home should always reflect your personality and personality of your partner. So when it comes to decoration and bringing small elements to it you both should be involved.

For example: if one of the partners is a painter there should be some elements of art or your partner's work, things he or she likes the most and if your partner is into samurai swords you should have some on display. And so on.

If you have any prizes or diplomas you should have them somewhere you can see them (if you enjoy seeing them of course).

Decorating the living space is a taste thing and everybody decides how to decorate it on their own.

But don't forget to check with your partner when you bring something new in the house or are thinking of getting rid of something so you avoid nasty surprises. Remember that the house you live in is your special place first and everything else afterwards. Work together to make it your special space.

DIY

and refurbishing the house

DIY is inescapable. It happens to everybody and it happens at least twice a year if not more often. Whatever you need to fix, re-new, re-paint in order to save some cash couples start doing things themselves and as it happens end up having an argument which can even lead to splitting up in some

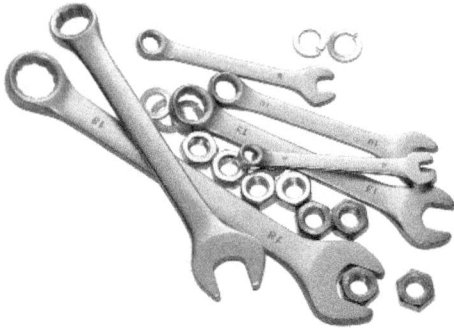

cases. Extreme as this may sound ir still happens more often than it should and you should be aware of it.

When you are doing your house up yourself it is always very stressful and all the negative energy goes to whoever happens to be near at the moment – and usually it happens to be your partner.

It's normal and it's explainable that you get stressed and short tempered. But it is not normal to have an argument over that. The easiest way to get into that kind of situation is to get stressed. Let's talk about how not to end up fighting over timetables and missing brushes first.

How to escape an argument during the DIY season

Planning and being prepared

Every time you plan to do something in the house with your partner you need to PLAN. Yes, this is something a lot of people just don't do, they never plan and they let things get out of control. Sometimes you can get carried away and go ahead doing things without having the tools to finish the job, some people even start knocking down walls and then they live in an after-a-nuclear-explosion-look house for weeks (or even months). This is something you can easily get into just by starting to fix a single tile in the kitchen (when a whole block of tiles falls off the wall).

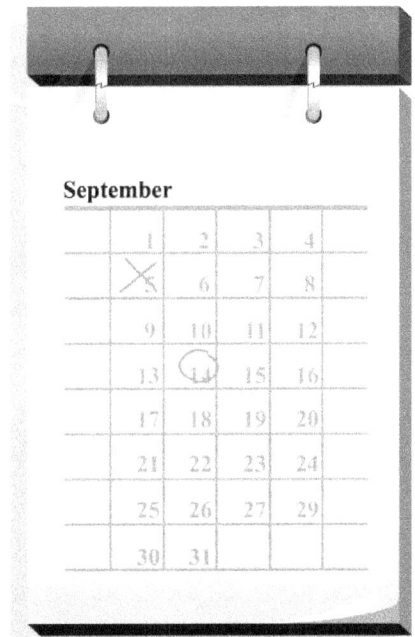

September

1	2	3	4
5	6	7	8
9	10	11	12
13	14	15	16
17	18	19	20
21	22	23	24
25	26	27	29
30	31		

To avoid incidents like that you need to make sure that you have everything you need and a little bit more than you need. DIY never goes smoothly and that's a fact. So be prepared for things to go wrong, have extra parts and extra paint, and have wiping and cleaning stuff by your side while working. Be prepared that you probably will not finish anything in time.

Do your research

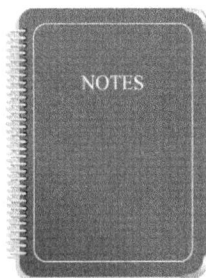

Make sure you have all the information needed for the work you are planning to do. Most DIY stores will have free leaflets available and you can always ask expert advice. Sometimes something really small may take quite some time to put together when it looked like it was going to be no more than a 5-minute-job so it's good to get all the information possible on the subject BEFORE you start anything.

Do your research online, Google it, ask in forums. The internet is your best friend when it comes to Doing Things Yourself. There are also a lot of new gadgets coming on the market every year so it would be wise of you to check them out, some of them canmake the job and your life a lot easier.

You can listen to your friends and family's advice as well but don't rely on it too much. Whatever you are planning to do always recheck it online or check with someone who does it for a living (if possible).

Work out your budget

The reason you are doing your house up yourself is to save money so be reasonable in how you spend money. You don't want to end up getting a loan in the middle of the process of putting your bathroom in when you run out of money. So whatever you are able to spend you have to make sure you have this money and you have a little bit extra for the emergency cases. Don't forget that you will still need to have money for living after you finish doing your house up.

Be reasonable

If you can clearly see that you can't afford to paint the whole house in one go and there may not be enough paint you leave it for later. When it comes to painting for example you need to have more paint than you will actually use because after you finish painting you will still need to use the same paint from the same mix from the factory in case you need to renew the paint later on. So it's never "it's just a paintbrush and bucket of paint I need".

REMEMBER :

- Stress and aggression are always in the air when you are doing something and it needs both of you to have a let bygones be bygones strategy in place that will defuse potentially explosive situations.
- Everything takes too long.
- There are no right tools available.
- There is not enough material to work with.

So you always make sure you have plenty of time even for things to go wrong and you are prepared to spend sometime fixing things, you always have the right tools (because you have already done your research) and you have enough money for the material (paint, wallpapers, tiles etc) and a little bit on top of that if necessary. Then the DIY season can become enjoyable for both of you in the end.

After all that's why you are going into all this trouble in the first place – you are building a house for two of you. Always remember that having unfinished work around you is much worse than not starting doing anything at all. So unless you are both prepared to wait for the next phase of work for a week or a month you don't get into DIY at all.

Always remember it's just things. Your relationship matters much more.

ALWAYS REMEMBER:

• You are doing it for yourself and your partner and not for somebody else (to impress your friends and neighbours for instance).

• You are doing it to improve your quality of life and to make your relationship and life together better so it has to be your mutual decision on every little thing you bring in your house (like the colour of the walls for example – you both need to like it).

Pushing your partner to start refurbishing the house

It's a common mistake to push your partner to do what they may not want to do in order for them to please you. As a result many couples split up over this. When you start pushing your partner to take action and start changing the house you both live in you have a problem. If your partner is happy living with you in the house you are in and doesn't want to change anything just yet the first thing you do is you talk. You discuss the possibility of renewing it bit by bit (if it's really what you want) and find compromises.

But before even that you should ask yourself: is it the house I am not happy about or is it my partner? And you have to answer honestly. Many people have fallen in that trap when they were hoping to change the house = change their life = change their partner. They were not happy with their relationship and they thought that a new wallpaper could save it… It never does.

So if you are having problems over your living space you have a problem and you need to solve it. The house and the space are only enjoyable for both of you if you are already happy with each other and only in this case can you start any DIY work. If you have problems, if you argue a lot then doing DIY together will only finish it for both of you.

It's never the house. It's you!

House decoration

Little bits create a picture and details always matter. Some people think that small things like candles and napkins is something you buy on a bulk sale and only so that you can fill the space. But they are wrong.

Little things like that are important because they create a certain atmosphere in your house so that you feel cosy there and you feel at home. It is also important that you choose these 'little' things together no matter how little they may seem to be. They are after all part of the 'character' you are creating for the space you live in.

Little things like:

Candles
Lights
Scent sticks and oils
Variety of napkins
Fresh flowers
Pillows and cushions
Coasters
Frames with photographs
Pictures

Generally you need to surround yourself with things you like and enjoy looking at. For example, a lot of people keep lots of different cups in the draw which don't match, they are very old and some of them were gifts. You don't notice these things. You certainly don't enjoy using them. But when you are living together you should enjoy every minute of it life is too short to allow things to become tasteless and joyless.

When you are having breakfast or lunch or dinner you can turn it into a little celebration every day and every time. It costs so little and it takes so little time but how much you gain beacuse of this!

Place some lovely napkins with a cheerful pattern on the breakfast table (take or make the time to have breakfast together), use nice and stylish glasses, decorate the meal with greenery and fruit. Have candles if it's dinner time and flowers if it's early breakfast.

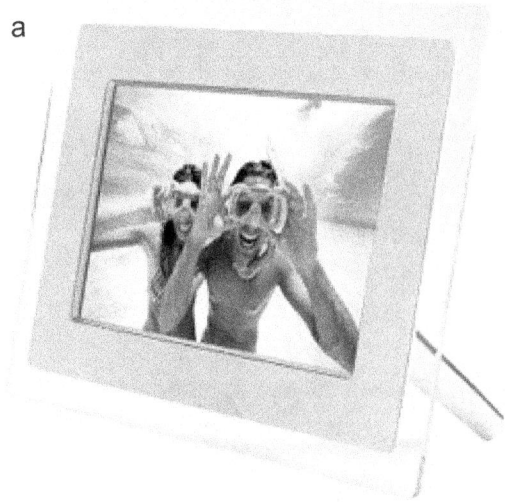

Enjoy having your meal with your partner because it is a little celebration of your life together, another happy day of your life.

Opening up and sharing feelings

Sometimes because we don't talk we create a problem in our heads and keep thinking in the wrong direction about something the other person said or did. But the answer could be very simple and totally different from our own conclusion. That's why you always need to talk with your partner about anything which is not clear in your relationship, in your actions or something which one of you has said. Sometimes it can be difficult but the alternative of not-knowing and creating a problem out of nothing based on circumstantial evidence is much worse.

Analyse yourself: Do you feel that you can't ask your partner about something sensitive for both of you? Do you feel you can't tell your partner about a problem you are facing because you feel you will look bad in your partner's eyes?

Opening up is always difficult especially when strong feelings are involved out of fear of getting hurt. But if you can't open up with the person you are planning to spend your life with who are you going to open up with? Being together, sharing your lives mean more than just sharing a few square meters of space! You share your feelings, your worries as well as happy moments; you support and comfort each other when the hard time comes. And in order to do all these things you need to be able to communicate openly and easily with your partner no matter what the subject is about and no matter how sensitive it is.

Being open with someone is not easy and it does take time to open up, but if you really want to be happy with your partner you can't hold anything back. If you have hidden worries, if you are not sure about something or even angry with your partner over something you have to talk about it as soon as possible.

Most common things

which are difficult to share

Self image problems

Most of us have them no matter how good we are at hiding them. It can be some natural imperfections (like a big nose, big ears or something similar), it can be speech problems or most common these days – worries about being overweight. People find it difficult to share things like that especially with someone they are attracted to. The problem exists in the first place only because of a lack of self-confidence.

Solution

Don't be afraid to express your feelings, joke about it and try to open up as much as possible. The fear itself usually is much worse than the situation itself. If your partner is already with you and loves you why do you think that is? So you can't keep creating a problem which might be an imaginary issue. Be brave and share.

Financial arrangement problem

Not very many people can talk easily about money once they enter a serious relationship. There can be all sorts of problems and most common of them is not trusting each other when it comes to spending money and earning abilities. You can't possibly earn the same amount and one of you probably will earn more than the other. And there is also the case of you having common budget as you both have common bills to pay.

Solutions

First of all, you must always remember that it really doesn't matter who earns how much as it's not the money you are with each other for. At the end of the day you have a common 'pocket' for both incomes. And this is another issue as some people have separate incomes and take care of the bills separately. It's wrong though it may seem practical. Sometimes partners even don't know how much each other earns! Think about it: if you are living together, if you are building your life together and planning to stay together for a long time why would you have secrets from each other? So it's important that you both sit down and discuss your financial situation so you both know what's going on and what you can rely on: write down all the expenses and bills you have to pay monthly and the sums you spend on food and household expenses so you are aware where the money goes. That will help you to avoid mistrust in your relationship on a financial basis. It's silly to ruin your feelings for each other over money don't you think? Never keep your partner in the dark when it comes to money as it affects both of you and the other person has a right to know.

The Jealousy problem

We always feel jealous when we are in love and it's normal. What is not normal is going mad over that and not talking about it. You can feel jealous of an ex-partner, a child, a friend and even a pet or a thing like a hobby. You can also make your partner jealous of something or somebody and may not even know about it. Jealously is always corrosive in a relationship. It has a way of getting completely out of control so never 'toy' with your partner's feelings this way just so you can prove to yourself how much the other person loves you.

Solution

First of all you need to analyze the situation and talk about it. Then you need to reassure your partner that there is no reason to feel jealous because you are there for him (or her) and no one else. There is no reason for you to keep in contact with your EXs so it will be better for both of you to have no contact with your previous lovers. After all once you had intimate contact with somebody you can't be friends and that's just how it is. Try not to give reasons for jealousy even to make sure your partner loves you. Never test your partner that way and never use it to get back at him (or her). It's cruel and it's never about love.

The Sex question

You'll be surprised. But a lot of couples are not comfortable talking about their sexual preferences with each other. Sometimes they feel their partner won't understand and will think of them as perverts. Women more often fake orgasms just to keep their partner happy and men would never ask their partner something they think their lover would object to.

Solution

It is most important that you do talk no matter how difficult it is. You have to do it. Sex may be not the most important thing in any relationship but it is very important for both of you to be satisfied. If you are not satisfied as time passes it will get only worse and you will start blaming your partner in causing that. Sexual dissatisfaction on its own is not a deal-breaker but it becomes the catalyst which causes many relationships to start developing cracks.

How to break the ice

Discuss things you see on TV or stories about other people to discover what your partner thinks and feels about something in particular.

Guide your partner with moaning during sex to let him (or her) know when you feel especially good.

Use petting to find your partner's most sensitive zones and remember them. Remember sex is all about intimacy, openess and trust as well as desire, lust and personal satisfaction. The trick is in attaining a balance that fulfils you and your partner in every way.

Agreements and expectations

Sometimes we really want to please our partner and we agree on something we are not really happy about. It can be a big buy or a holiday or anything like that. We think that by doing that we are making our partner happy. Well it is logical isn't it? You think if you do what your partner wants to do he (or she) will be happy. But it's wrong.

First of all you don't know what your partner really thinks of the proposed thing, maybe the whole intention is to make you happy. That's why you always need to talk about it. You need to find out why your partner wants to do or experience something and then analyse yourself and think why you don't.

Analyse yourself: Maybe you don't want to do something with your partner because you don't want to spend time together? You need to catch that kind of feeling before it is too late. If there is a problem in your relationship it will only get worse in time and without resolving it will never go away.

If you are talking about a big buy and you are not happy about it because your finances cannot allow it you also need to talk about it. Nothing can be worth the anger and your disappointment in your partner's "inability to calculate and do simple math". After all, your partner cannot be even aware of your financial difficulties and only thinks that this buy will make you both happy. If you sit down and talk about it you can explain the situation and you can both decide when you will be able to buy the desirable object (or go on holiday). So that way you both will be happy.

T I P : Never blame your partner for misunderstanding or misjudgements when you explain why you can't do something right now or in nearest future. When you explain things you need to make sure your partner is comfortable and not feeling bad about the proposal. Explain that you can still do it and you will be happy to do it but just not right now. And smile. Explaining things like this sounds like we need to be apologetic about personal perceived failings. It's not the case, but it does make for tenses moments which is why it's important to smile.

Don't feel bad that your partner has said or done something you never expected him (or her) to. It's absolutely normal to go along with a mood on a good day or just have something in mind and spell it out and then be rebuffed. First thing you should do is to think: Would she (or he) want to upset me? Of course not! And the reason usually is simply not knowing what was in your head at that moment. So the first thing you need to do is share your worries with your partner so you are both aware of the situation.

You would hate your partner being happy, singing and dancing around you when you have a head full of unresolved problems. How bad does that sound? That's why you always need to share not just happy moments but your problems as well. Talk about it and maybe together you can find the perfect solution.

The trust

Big and small promises

It is important that both of you stick to your word. It's important to build a trust between the two of you. If you can't trust each other who can you trust then? You can't make a promise and then never remember about it because the other person will feel betrayed. It doesn't matter if it's a big promise or a small promise to go for a walk or to do something in the house, if you gave it you need to stick to it no matter what. Because if you don't the other person will know that he (or she) can't trust your word.

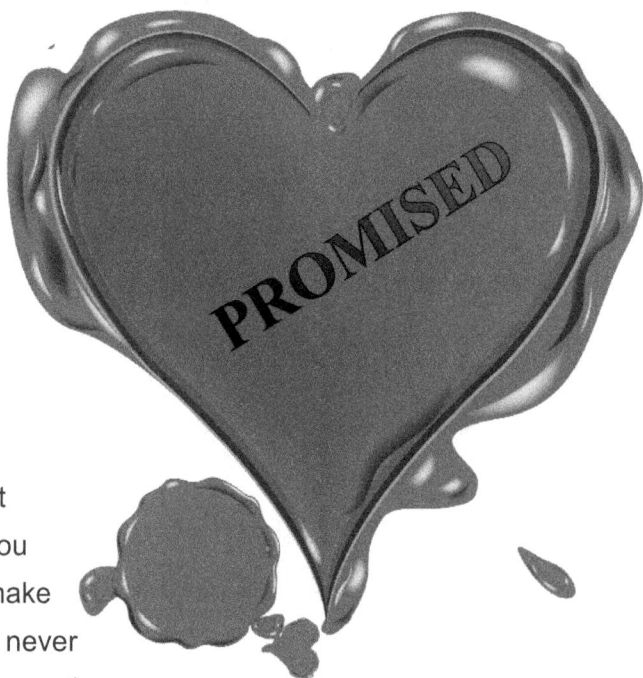

So it doesn't matter if you are too busy or you think that the thing you have promised doesn't really mean a lot you still need to do it or at least tell the other person that you can't do it right now and you will do it later (always specify the time).

Imagine: you promised to do something in the house and the other person is waiting for you to do it. You forget about what you have promised because you have been too busy but the other person is still waiting and getting frustrated and beginning to think that you will never do it. And then you get frustrated that your partner reminds you about the promise or gets on your case: "Oh I never expected you to do it! It's fine, it's fine…" One of *those* "FINE". That's how huge arguments start.

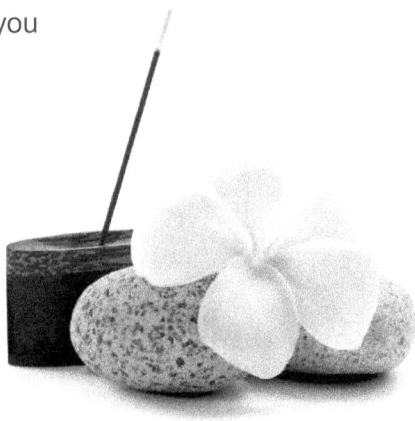

A simple notice on the delay and a brief discussion on when it will be done could prevent the whole thing. If you keep track of things you are planning to do it can help a lot! Have a promise list next to your working to-do's and you will never forget a simple small task for your beloved, again.

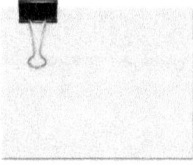

Note: When you get frustrated and your partner reminds you about something you haven't done yet when you promised don't get angry and yell. That's the worst reaction you can have. Be calm and always think that other person doesn't mean to make you feel guilty or uncomfortable; your partner only does it because he or she feels non-important and forgotten. The only reaction you will get if you yell will be: "I will never ask you to do anything again, ever again!"

Giving an opportunity

Even when you know that your partner is hopeless in something you still need to give him (or her) a chance because you can't learn and improve without actual practice. It doesn't matter if your partner will fail again and again it is all part of the learning process. And in this case you need to be supportive and try to cheer your partner up.

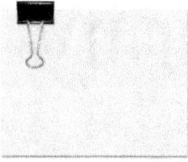

Note: Never lie and say that your partner has done an excellent job because that way you give your partner confidence that there is no need for improvement. It's going to get only worse in time if you let it go.

You shouldn't stop your partner from doing something you know is not going to work if your partner is excited about the idea. If you can avoid the crisis by helping them do it but don't criticise every time your partner makes a mistake.

It can be anything from DIY to cooking it doesn't matter what it is but it is your first responsibility to trust your partner, support the initiative and the most important thing is to trust them doing things.

Just think: how can your partner learn to cook if you never give him (or her) an opportunity to do it?

Solution

Practise doing the cooking together. Make it fun and enjoyable. Find cookery books, DVD with cooking course, practise together. Give them a chance! Help and support. If your partner gets stressed during the process offer your help.

Yeah, maybe it won't be perfect and the entire thing will be wrecked (and maybe you knew it from the beginning) but so what? It's only things. Look on the bright side: your partner tried and failed maybe he (or she) won't try to do it again or maybe this time he (or she) learnt how to do it right.

You on other hand have an opportunity to show your partner how really deeply you love him (or her) by saying:

• It doesn't matter at all, such a small thing! Happens with everybody! Don't even think about it.
• I am really proud of you, you have done very well. I am sure next time you will do even better. You are improving already. In case of broken or damaged things ignore them (they are just things after all, aren't they?) - suggest:

Let's go and get another one (or – We will get another one)
It's cool. I never liked it anyway :)

And next time something similar happens to you your partner will remember it and will support you back.

That's how you both learn to support each other and just let things go. There is no point in having an argument over broken things or jobs being done wrong. You are not enemies to have no scores and points to gain against each other. Take it easier and you will see that the relationship gets better and you are getting along much easier.

The Control question

Where are you and when are you going to be back?

Business meetings, friends and simply staying somewhere longer than he or she is supposed to can piss you off big time but remember: ringing up every 5 minutes demanding the location and estimated time of arrival is not good for either of you. Your partner may feel that you are trying to control him (or her) and instead of coming back home happy and relieved will be angry and unhappy with the situation. And home has to be a special place, safe and welcoming. Otherwise why would you want to go back there?

Very few people can actually time things to a minute and you always need to remember that no matter how bad you

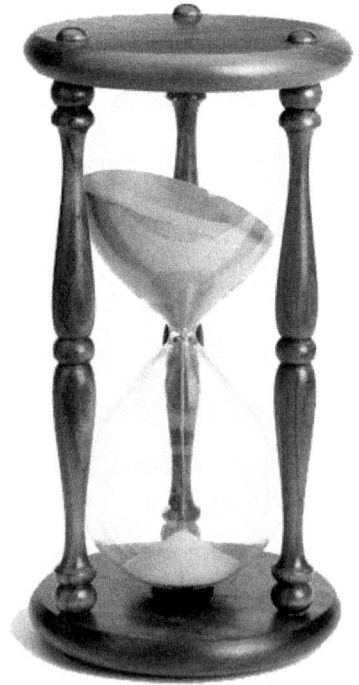

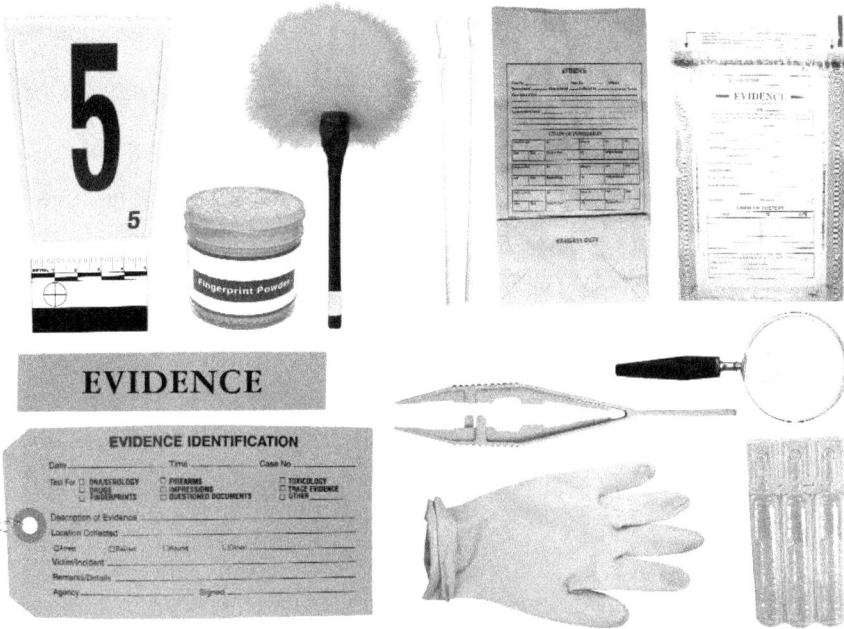

feel you can never express it on the phone. If it happens too often and it's not business related than you can discuss it tet-a-tet with your partner and agree always to text or call each other in case of a delay or complications at work.

When you don't talk you create a huge problem. You don't tell your partner that you feel bad and keep building it up inside you and your partner thinks that you simply don't care.

Control over our partners is something we all would love to have because it gives us complete peace of mind, but the only control you can afford to have in order to have in a good Relationship is self-control.

Remember that the forbidden fruit is always incredibly attractive just because it is forbidden. So spying on your partner, demanding his or her location in a particular moment will only annoy the hell out of them and may seed a thought that there may be someone else who will be more understanding than you.

Being jealous never helped anybody. You must always treat your partner with respect, the same respect you expect in return. Give your partner full freedom in terms of meeting friends and going partying with co-workers. All your really need in the end is for him or her is to come back home to your warm bed.

If you are not sure about them, have doubts and really think your partner is cheating then don't be afraid to talk about it ask the question in a straightforward manner. You never get down to the level where you are spying and investigating on a daily basis sniffing your partner's clothes, checking receipts and parking tickets.

If your partner really is cheating you will eventually find out and it will be over between the two of you. But if he (or she) is not you may only provoke him (or her) to do that.

There always has to be a welcoming home to come back to. People cheat and lie usually because there are problems at home and they need to escape that environment. It's never just about sex. In most cases affairs start exactly because one of the partners was too controlling.

Reality check

If your partner wants to leave you he (or she) will. And you can only make it worse by checking up and investigating when your partner is away and complaining about where they have been and how long they have taken after your partner is back home. Why would your partner want to come back to you? So that he (or she) can listen to your complaints again and again?

Relationships end because people don't give each other breathing space!

Respecting a person you are living with is almost as important as loving them. You see love is very egotistical in most cases. You always want another person for yourself even if you truly believe and do everything just for the other's person happiness.

But love is very selfish and what we would really like is to own the other person. But we don't and this is something not very many people understand.

Some are convinced that marriage for example gives you the right to demand pretty much anything at all and practically it's like signing a Soul Owning pact. Wrong. Marriage is a social act where you are saying to the world (and your government) that you are committed to have a family together. But it doesn't give you any right to treat your partner as your property. It doesn't give you a lifetime insurance that your partner won't cheat and lie and it definitely doesn't give you his (or her) heart forever.

Love is a very gentle and vulnerable feeling which is really easy to lose. In some cases (if not most) people just become good friends without even realizing that. They live like that for years till the very end unless one of the partners will meet somebody who will fire him (or her) up again and leave the friend-like relationship for the long-forgotten feeling of love and excitement.

Dealing with arguments

Who should say "I am sorry" first and does it really matter?

Everybody has arguments. Even perfect couples every so often get into a fight over silly things. It can be just because of being in a bad mood or stress or a simple misunderstanding. The cause is irrelevant because the most important thing is to always remember that you are fighting with someone you love and stop it right there. Sometimes even a kiss or a hug will be enough to stop any argument. Unfortunately instead in most cases there are words flying from one side to the other and back spreading death and destruction, hurting and making us miserable. And what is it all for? After that you will go somewhere and go through the argument again and again on your own now feeling worse and worse every minute.

There are two very common scenarios: **making up in bed** the same evening or **pretending that nothing happened the next morning**.

Both are unacceptable!

In both cases you are trying to escape from resolving the problem instead of solving it. The next time another issue will come up it will be wired up with the previous accident as well working just like a snowball coming down the mountain. Problems don't go away if you pretend they don't exist, and avoiding solving them is no solution. That's why you always need to talk.

Here goes the recipe

First of all you need to calm down and stay on your own for at least 15 minutes. Never try to solve the argument immediately if you are not completely calm. But never leave it for hours either as it can only make the situation worse in your and your partner's heads (you begin to remember old arguments and mistakes totally irrelevant for this particular case but it just keeps winding you up).

It doesn't matter who says "I am sorry" first. It doesn't mean that you lose. Once you understand that there can be no winners in the relationship of two people in love you will cut down by 50% the number of arguments you could have with the one you love. Nothing in the world is worth losing someone you love because you couldn't agree on something or because you couldn't find the 'guilty party' in an argument.

Remember: To make an argument you need two people. It says it all.

No matter how bad you feel you always think that the other person is not feeling great right now either. Making peace and resolving the issue is always the best policy.

So:

• Phrase the problem and describe it, write it down if necessary.

• Make sure you both understand the problem and you are talking about the same thing.

• Find a logical solution and make compromises if necessary.

• And remember: it is important that you talk about the problem there and then and find the root of it so you don't have to cross it again and again in the future.

What you shouldn't do after the argument

• Walk away and come back in the morning, as you may come back into an empty house or to a dead body.

• Start packing suitcases and threatening to leave (go to your mum, hotel etc). This is emotional blackmail and you can never use it against someone you love. Otherwise you can't really call it love, can you?

• Damage the objects around (throw chairs, break dishes). Aggression never solves anything. It helps you to get rid of some steam (so does meditation and just some time spent alone) but it threatens your partner and just makes the situation worst. Never mind the fact you are breaking things.

• Fighting

The way you look at home reflects the way you feel about the person you are with

The way you look does matter. If you go round the house dressed in an old bath robe and you don't care about your looks when your partner is looking you have a problem. Even if you have spent together 10 years and know every nasty little bit of each other it doesn't mean that you should forget about how you look around the house. First of all it works at a psychological level where you stop seeing your partner as a sexually attractive person and a person who is worth making an effort for. It happens and it happens quite often and it an lead to deep-seated problems in your relationship.

The reason people don't notice it in time is because it kind of happens gradually and when they realize it, it is already too late. If they ever realize at all. This is one of the reasons why people cheat on each other. They need to feel wanted and loved (in whatever meaning) and it's never just about having a sexual experience with another person.

But I am not saying that you should constantly have evening make-up on or be dressed up in a suit. But wearing sexy clothes, fresh clothes, being cleanly shaven and smiling every so often will make a big difference.

Being in shape is also important. If you don't respect yourself and your body why do you expect the other person to respect and love you? The typical women question is: will you love me if I will get fat? – Yes honey – is the reply they expect. But really it doesn't matter what the reply is, because you never let yourself go because sexual attraction between two loving people is a very important thing. Otherwise in time you will just become good friends living together (best case scenario) but you will start looking for sex outside your relationship. Just to feel wanted again.

Exercise together, join the gym, or go for a morning run. Exercise can be very enjoyable especially if you have your partner exercising with you, supporting you and just keeping you company.

A T I P : If you can't make a time for exercise you can still exercise because every little bit counts. If you do 10 sit-ups and 5 press-ups before you go to bed or early in the morning and you do it every day at the end of the week you will have 100 sit-ups and 35 press-ups done which is just like spending one hour at the gym.

Every little bit helps.

Respecting the other person is not just respecting their talents and personal freedoms. It's also making an effort when it comes to things around and about yourself. That means looking after yourself and making sure you are always fresh and welcoming for a hug and kiss. If you wonder why your partner stopped kissing you every so often with no reason at all look in the mirror and ask yourself "Would I kiss myself?". After all we all want our partners to be the best of what they can be so we should apply the same logic to ourselves.

You probably heard a popular story: They got married - she put weight on and you can never see her smiling; he stopped shaving and wears dirty clothes. They argue a lot and have affairs.

Well, it happens very often, people just stop trying for each other. Of cause it's never just about looks. Problems about looks are more a result of people shutting each other out but the way each person looks also plays a role. For some reason princes and princesses once they become wives and husbands stop making an effort for each other. That's when it stops being a fairy tale…

So… the best you can do is:

• Even if you are bored and tired you still stay fresh and clean at home, clean shaven and smell nice.

• Always wear your best clothes. It's just clothes clothes are there for you to wear and not to collect dust on the shelves. After all you can buy new clothes but you can't buy a new relationship. Also you will feel better yourself if you wear nice things at home. Never wear old robes and ancient t-shirts! The way your look for your partner is even more important than when you go to work. A new job is easier to find than a loving partner.

• Smile. How little people smile when they are at home. You don't need to have a reason to give your partner a smile or blow them kiss.

So do it as often as possible.

My friends, your friends

Friends, friends, friends… Sometimes they can be your worst enemies since some couples are so eager to discuss their relationship with their friends. What a mistake that is. No matter how things are between you and your partner your friends' opinion will only harm it. Why would you generally want their opinion about your relationship? It's your relationship.

If it's not going very well between you and your beloved your friends will only try to protect you or give you advice on how to find somebody "better". You can't blame them they are only trying to do their best for you.

And if it's going well you never give your friends any details about your personal life. That's why it's personal. If you start yelling about your private life at every street corner then it will stop being private and personal. And you will feel it. So no matter what's going on between you and your partner it has to stay between the two of you. You need to discuss it if there is a problem and solve it. But there can be only two of you involved.

Imagine: you are telling your friends that things are not going well for you in bed (for example) and next thing – you have solved the problem with your partner. But your friends already knew there was a problem. You cannot erase their memories… and you will not feel comfortable with them anymore.

Sometimes one of the partners feels very insecure when the other leaves for a friends' night out. It can be jealousy or just the fear that they might do something to harm the relationship. As a matter of fact the latter does happen very often.

Your friends never want you to stay away from them and the fact that you are having a good relationship and you are spending more time at home and not in their company can make them do and say things which will not work for your relationship.

After all not everybody has a partner and not everybody is happy in their own relationship so they try to spread the misery. You need to be able to see it and escape it.

When you are in a serious relationship the best you can do is to join yours and your partner's friends and make them your mutual friends. It's not an easy task but it solves a lot of problems. Invite them in for dinner; go on holiday together, go to the cinema and so on. That way both parts can get to know each other better.

It can be difficult sometimes but the alternative is worse as if your relationship gets better you won't have time for "just your friends" and you could even lose them.

Comparing

Just like you can't have somebody else's life you can't have somebody else's relationship. Have you ever caught yourself looking around and comparing your partner to somebody else's and wishing that he or she would be: stronger, smarter, taller, richer?

Apparently a lot of people do it all the time. But the thing is that if you really want your partner to change and become somebody else it's not your partner you are in love with but a picture you have drawn in your head.

If you really love somebody you don't want them to change. You want them to develop.

Comparing yourself with your friends and neighbours

Your friends can look more wealthy or happier but as it happens it can be just the looks and nothing more. Very few people are actually happy together but they don't want the rest of the world to know about it. So on the surface they can present a picture of endless happiness and success when like everybody else they have problems. Remember that.

We all want to look successful in somebody else's eyes. It's natural and it's socially acceptable. What isn't normal is for you to compare your relationship and your life to theirs.

Everybody has problems and no one is exceptional.

If you are trying to make your relationship better and you are trying to make it work you never rely on and never compare it to somebody next door.

Comparing your life with that of movie-stars

This is easy. It's a movie and you can't have your life and your relationship as beautiful and faultless as on the screen. Yet some people try. The sooner you realize that your life is your life and the movie is just a movie the sooner your relationship will become more enjoyable and trouble-free.

People who keep looking for examples to live their life by are trapped in a world of clones; they get so busy looking for a template to live their life so they never do live their life and as a result they lose their loved one in the early stages when they could just simply enjoy their happiness and their time together.

Trying to make yourself and your partner better using somebody's example is good but not when it's just blind copying. And this is where you need to understand the difference.

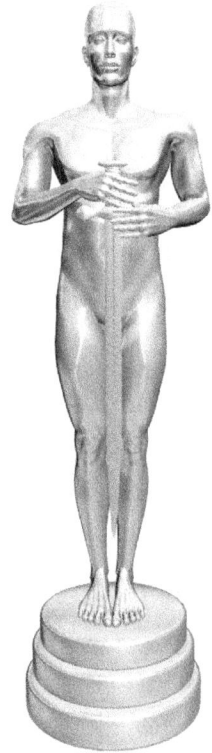

For example

You know that somebody is very driven and always gets who he wants so normally you would want your partner to be the same.

Wrong

It's not right to make your partner feel inferior by saying "Look at Mr Johnson how successful he is! Why can't you be like him?" The normal reaction to that is most probably anger. You partner will feel angry because you are comparing him (or her) to somebody else they may not even like and/or simply be jealous of the fact that you like somebody else.

Right

Is to say how good your partner is in something you want him to improve and give a few suggestions on how to make it even better. You never tell your partner that he (or she) is really bad in something and you want them to change. You inspire, you help, you suggest. If you want your partner to change and to become better you make him (or her) to want it himself (herself).

Making love
Feel it and do it
Talk about it

Most important thing in bed is to be natural and to open up. That's why so many married men go to prostitutes: there they can be themselves that's what they are paying for. Why not receive the same thing at home?

How often do you make love? Two-three times a day? Twice a week? Once a year?

How much time do you spend before the actual act and after? Cuddling and hugging is a very important part of bonding and sex itself. Spontaneous and passionate sex is good but it can be like that all the time.

How often do you talk about sex? It's important that you share your

preferences and your views on all sexual aspects with your partner in order to be able to understand each other better and understand each other's needs. You need to cover all the possibilities and all the options you have.

The most important thing is to make sure you both can easily talk about pretty much anything when it comes to sex. That you can share anything at all and can openly tell about your needs.

So…there are things you can to help you and your partner in this.

• go shopping in a sex shop (even if you have no intention of buying anything) so that you can look at all the varieties of toys and general equipment on offer.

• go online and surf the net for sex stories so that you can talk about them and have a laugh and explore this part of your sexuality.

• play sex games like strip poker.

If you find it difficult to open up just like that then get drunk. It's much easier to talk about sex when you are not quite sober. You can have a glass of wine with candle light so that it's only the two of you and all your fantasies.

Play a game

You take turns and tell each other stories. Every story starts with "Lady Hamilton…" and "Sir Gilmore…" and there use your imagination. What did they do and how did it end….

What you never-ever do:

You never discuss your love life before you met. Especially if it was good… You don't want your partner to feel jealous or feel second-best so keep your sex-life with other people to yourself. The stories from your past will only provoke your partner to compete with your EXs.

Sweet Ideas

Sweet names and notes

It is important that you call each other with sweet names even if you think it's silly. Because nothing between the two of you can ever be silly. Not just because it is romantic but it also helps you to express your feelings in one-two words during the day. You don't have to make other people uncomfortable in public, it will be just like secret words only for the two of you.

You can leave notes to each other during the day even if you are spending it together. Leave a note in the bathroom with a smile on it.

Breakfast in bed

It's everybody's dream and once you are talking about a romantic gesture everybody remembers "breakfast in bed" but very few actually do it. Why? Maybe because they think it's too common or maybe they just forget and yet and yet it's a simple and elegant way to let somebody know how you feel about them. It takes no time at all to place a cup of coffee and a croissant next to your beloved before he (or she) wakes up. It's simple and it works.

Cookies and milk

Nobody likes being ill but it happens and it is terrible watching your loved one being ill. But you can make it better for your partner showing him (or her) how much you care. It's not just calling a doctor and buying the medicine. It's also your cheering up and things you do apart from the standard procedure. You can make some chocolate cookies with milk for your partner and bring it to the 'patient's' bed.

Chicken soup will work as well as cookies if you are on the healthy side. What does matter is that you do it yourself; you don't go and just buy it ready but make it with your own hands. It means a lot and it shows a lot.

Flying a kite

It's a windy gray day? And it happened to be Sunday? Perfect! You can get a kite (Almost any supermarket will sell it – check out the kid's section) or you can make one yourself (look for a tutorial online). You can write little messages on your kite before you fly it and then let it go free. There is a certain amount of trust involved when you let your partner fly a kite. In fact, what's stopping you from getting two kites?

Discover a new taste together

You can both try a new cuisine by fishing out exotic recipes online or you can take off and go to a restaurant you have never tried before.

Cooking for each other and being excited about it is just what the doctor has prescribed. Even if things go wrong you can always order something in and have a Chinese meal after all.

Every couple's must-have list

Digital Photo Camera

Nobody remembers how awkward it was staying in the doorway forever waiting for somebody to take a picture while you are holding the gifts for the occasion but everybody likes looking at the shots afterwards. Take as many pictures as possible even if you are just going for a walk together. Buy a small camera which fits in your pocket or smallest handbag so you always have it with you. Take pictures of places and generally everything you think will help you to remember the places where you have been together.

Two matching coffee/tea cups

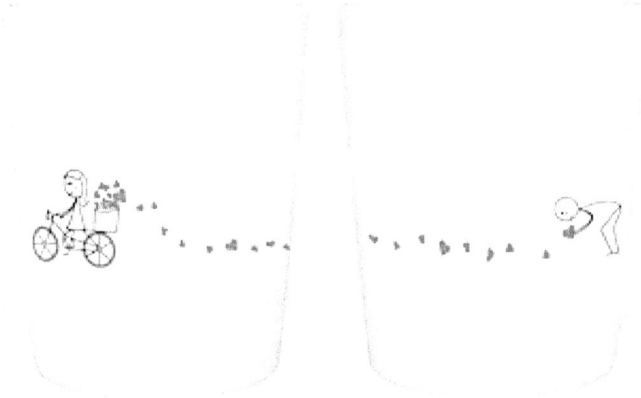

You should have two matching coffee or tea cups you use all the time. But they have to match and if possible have your names on them. You can order special cups for each other where you can write a little love message. The idea is that coffee or tea is something you do together. When at home it becomes personal and shared and part of your bonding ritual as a couple.

Have each other's photograph in your wallet/mobile phone wallper
It's not just sweet. It's having a little bit of your partner with you all the time. Think of it as a talisman of your love.

Your song

Every couple has a special song which reminds them about their feelings and makes them smile. It can be a song you heard when you first met or it can be a song you both used to listen to, or even a song which describes your feelings best. You should have a CD with it always around the house or an MP3 player at your computer so you can easily turn it on wherever you feel like it. You can also place it as a mobile phone ring tone for each other.

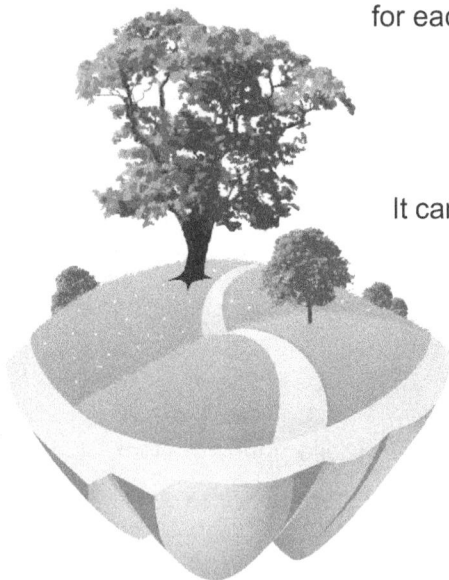

Your place

It can be your favourite restaurant or a bench in the park; it can even be a country. Any place you two associate with your relationship and being a couple can be your special place.

Satin sheets

These days you can have your satin bedding as regular bedding not just for the special occasion. It's romantic, beautiful and it's sexy. You can buy bright new satin sheets on eBay for as little as £12.

Your own cookery book

It is certain that you will both have special meals you like especially? Have you ever imagined that you could actually have a home menu that's uniquely your own? You can create one yourself with your own hands or create one using any graphic program on your computer.

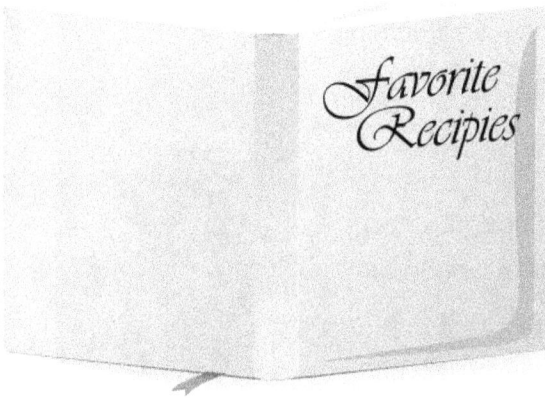

Towels with your initials

You can order to personalize your towels or you can do it yourself. Go for first letters of your names or your full names (ex. Ashley and Michael). Make them your own, add them to the growing list of things which create a sphere of uniqueness around you.

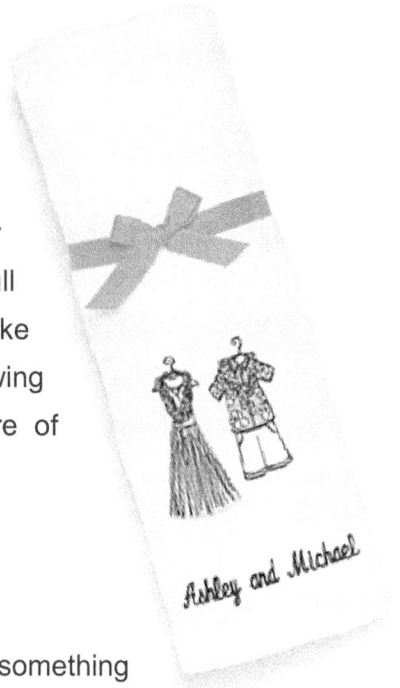

Massage oil

Some people think that a massage is something you give and receive once a year unless you go to a massage salon.

But really a massage is something you can give to each other all the time. It's a wonderful feeling touching your partner and finding out his (or her) pleasure spots. Giving pleasure sometimes can be even more enjoyable than receiving. You can buy a special massage oil with different flavours and make the night last forever for the two of you.

A Mascot!

Every couple must have a mascot! You can buy a toy together and it will become your relationship mascot. Keep it somewhere in the house where you can both see it. It's better if it will be a funny animal like the IKEA rat for example.

Gifts, presents, surprises

When was the last time you surprised your partner with a small gift without any reason or occasion? Most people think that these things are not important and they shouldn't waste their energy on doing something insignificant.

The thinking behind it is simple: why do you need to do anything special with no reason for your partner if your partner knows how you feel about him or her anyway?

Well, just knowing is never enough.
When there is no attention being paid to each other then the feeling between the two of you becomes a perfect ground for doubts and misreadings.

Gifts, surprises and little presents can deliver small messages of love and deep care. It's so easy and obvious that a lot of people manage to ignore it completely thinking it's too trivial to bother with and too obvious to even attempt.

As time passes we start to forget what it is like to make every day special when you are together with someone you love. In the end you may actually forget what loving feels like that's how un-special the day becomes. So in order to maintain it and keep it exciting you don't need to have a reason. You make up a reason and make it happen.

Flowers, sweets, little notes, little gifts like notebooks and pens, toys and seasonal things you can find in a nearest supermarket all these things can become a gift and can make your partner smile. These are little things but it's a big deal when it comes to giving them to each other.

When you are in love you want to give your beloved the whole world on a plate but once you are already together for some time you get other priorities in life. Everybody falls in that trap and in the end lose interest in each other. It's just not exciting and there is no passion left between you anymore.

But it doesn't have to be that way!

Surprise your partner, make them smile every day of your life, enjoy giving pleasure and sure enough your partner will pick it up too and will surprise you and answer with care in return.

What to give

It doesn't matter what it will be exactly but all gifts from you should follow two rules:

-        It has to be a surprise, you don't just agree on what you will buy for your partner's birthday or other occasion or even worst you just give them money. You have to find something and make it a surprise whatever it takes.

-        It has to have your personal touch. It can be an engraving or a note with a love poem, or love song. It has to have something which makes it a gift from you and not just something you went and bought and end of story. It has to have a meaning and thinking behind it depending on your partner's needs, interests and desires.

If it's a trip or a voucher make sure your partner will have something she or he can keep and remember about the event.

What not to give

-        You never buy something you like yourself and you never buy something you both will use around the house. It stops being a gift then.

-        You never buy something which will be consumed like a shaving pack or a deodorant.

-        You never buy wine and/or chocolates (you have friends for that pleasure) unless your partner is a collector and it's a rare thing you are giving them.

Receiving gifts

When we receive a gift we always say thank you. It's just how we've been taught to behave. And we always think that our beloved knows how really deeply grateful and happy we are. Well, apparently we always think that our partner will just read our mind and get the message. It never happens.

If you really care about what your partner has done for you then JUMP! LAUGH! SHOUT! SCREAM! Show your emotions, feelings! Hug and kiss.

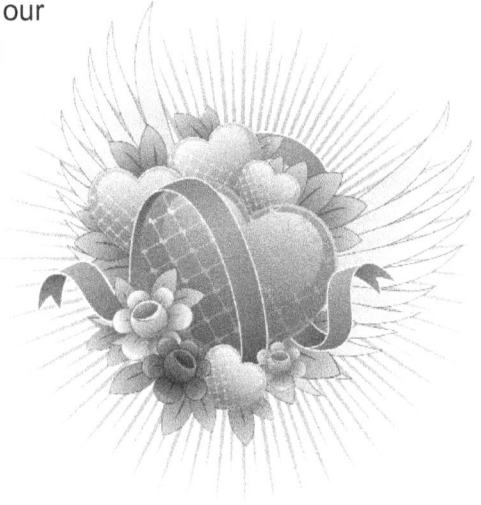

There is only one way to really express your feelings and let your partner know that the effort has been appreciated greatly. A simple thank you never inspires anybody and next time your partner will think twice before getting you something nice. It's not about being ungrateful it's about showing that you really enjoyed whatever your partner has done for you. Receiving gifts is not just "Oh, thank you, very nice of you" when it comes to someone you love. When you receive a gift from your partner let him\her know that it was really SOMETHING. Not because it was something outstanding or extremely expensive (it can be just a card after all) but because it came from him\her. That's what makes it special.

Flirting outside your relationship

Flirting outside your relationship…has never done any good to anyone. Yet there are people who enjoy flirting or it's just simply their nature. If you and/or your partner are into flirting there is still a way around it.

No you don't need to give it up. But you have to trust each other and what's more important keep each other informed when and what and most important with whom it has happened.

It can be flirting through Instant Messaging online or it can be flirting in real life with someone who is being extremely friendly. It doesn't matter till the point it becomes a secret from your partner then it becomes a problem.

It's part of our nature we all want to feel wanted and desired and that's where flirting comes from. And it doesn't mean we want every person we flirt with. We do it to prove to ourselves that other people are still interested in us; we do it to see their reaction.

Yet it can become a problem if you keep it secret and if you make your partner jealous.

And the other way round if you partner is a flirt and you are jealous it can cause a problem which if left unresolved can even lead to splitting up.

There are few things you must remember:

Be open no matter what and always tell your partner how you feel.

Share information about other people you communicate or\and flirt with. By doing that you reassure your partner that it's not serious and you want him or her to know that.

Give your partner enough attention as sometimes flirting starts where there is not enough attention from one of the partners.

If you can't control your feelings and jealousy talk about it but demand nothing. Let your partner know that you are upset and you think that his (or her) flirting with somebody hurts you.

The best you both can do when it comes to flirting is to become allies and make fun of it. Look at it as a hunt and talk about your successes. Inspire each other to flirt with other people and discuss their reaction together.

It can be something like a game. And two of you are the players but what's most important is that you are playing on the same side.

The Afterword

Love and The Second law of Thermodynamics

Imagine a beautiful garden and imagine if the owner of the garden stops watering it and stops giving it time and attention, pruning the roots of the plants and protecting them from pests. What is going to happen with this garden in the nearest future? It's going to die. The same thing happens with everything in the world - things we use, our houses, ourselves and our relationships.

This is the second law of thermodynamics: everything in the world degrades if we don't apply energy to maintain it and energy means thought and effort.

If you stop paying attention to things around you, you will lose them. And in order for things to keep working and keep in a good condition they need constant care and energy to be employed.

The same thing happens with your relationship. If you won't spend time with your partner and if you won't support your feelings for each other eventually they are going to die.

So no matter how safe you feel about your relationship at the moment you never let things go; this is like a boat and there are two of you in it you never let your boat go with the flow – you never know where you are going to end up. If you wait long enough you will end up at the end of the second law of thermodynamics.

It's important that you put energy in your relationship. It's important that you care.

Is this all?

Since the book was first written I have received countless emails, messages and letters some of them thanking them, some being complimentary and some of them asking for advice on specific issues they are facing.

Some have written in to ask why I could not include more examples and case studies in the book and others have questioned the lack of theory. The truth is that relationships are an inexact science and the theories behind the dynamics which govern them are constantly evolving and are being refined. When it comes to relationships there is no formula you can apply and no theory that will give you a vital insight in how to run it or how to save it if it is not going well. For all those who want some guidance and advice the only thing that really works is practical advice which can be implemented.

Anything else, and everything else is purely academic. Great to know and read about but really of very poor practical help. When I wrote this book my express purpose was for it to act as a practical guide which would evolve in its guidance with each reading helping you understand the dynamics with each reading as your own experience deepened.

To this end it has worked better than I had hoped, at least as far as the feedback I have jad through my website goes.

Many have also written to ask 'What Next?' and for that I am preparing a new book. But for those who are looking for the latest trends, research, hot issues and even relationship advice you can check out my website: www.ultimateguidetotheperfectrelationship.com.

Topical subjects

Controversial news

Hot issues!

Relationship advice

Ultimate Guide *to the* *Perfect Relationship*

WELCOME | ABOUT | PERFECT RELATIONSHIP BLOG | LOOK INSIDE | CONTENTS | TESTIMONIALS | BUY EBOOK | BUY PAPER COPY | MAIL ME

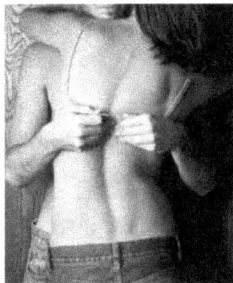

It's official there is no sisterhood!
A recent study carried out by researchers at the University of Aberdeen in the UK suggests that when it comes to solidarity women are really...

Self development and the development of your relationship
Self-development and the need for personal development is an obvious issue that affects many relationships, not least the ones which hit roc...

Is time spent apart good for a relationship?
Before we even begin to examine the question of whether time spent apart is good for a relationship let's get rid of all the clichés. Yes...

Virtual lives and offline relationships make for an uneasy mix
Hot off the press this morning was an article in London Times about a 40-year-old guy and his 28-year-old now ex-wife getting divorced when...

Is the notion of the sex bomb valid any longer?
I habitually write about specific aspects which affect relationships between couples and a look at whether the notion of the sex bomb is sti...

Should you sleep with a man on the first date?
When it comes to debating whether we should sleep with a guy on the first date it should be right up there with those two other constant points of the moral compass: 1. How small should your bikini be? and 2. What will my mother think? The point is that provided you are not hurting yourself or anybody else and you are not breaking any laws the question of morality in sleeping with a guy you like on the first date does not even come into it. Nor w...

read more ...

Over 120 pages packed with explanations, tips and a guide to having the perfect relationship

Each chapter helps you identify a specific area of your relationship. Understand why problems can occur and how and then know what you need to do in order to avoid them forever and solve them if you are experiencing them right now.

Download Paper Copy	$9.99 $14.99
Paper Copy Gift Edition	$49.99

LATEST ENTRIES | POPULAR

Is this the end of prostitution (and does it matter to your relationship?)

Should you sleep with a man on the first date?

It's official there is no sisterhood!

Self development and the development of your relationship

Is time spent apart good for a relationship?

Virtual lives and offline relationships make for an uneasy mix

Is the notion of the sex bomb valid any longer?

Updated daily!

www.ultimateguidetotheperfectrelationship.com.

Testimonials for Ultimate Guide to the Perfect Relationship

Dear Alisa, we wanted to say how this helped us love each other deeper. The chapter on "The way you look at home reflects the way you feel about the person you are with" helped us understand some issues we had been facing and resolve them. Thank you!!!!!!!!!!!!!! **Maria & Tom**

We worked through our Differences just like in the chapter in your book. There were some things in our relationship we never talked about and now, well, we really understand each other better.
Rod & Meegan

We both read this over a weekend. Alisa you got it spot on. It has not worked a miracle as all the issues we dealt with have not vanished overnight but at least we understand why they came up, we both understand why we had been mishandling them and we both understand that we are now travelling on the same path and share the same goals. That has been hugely important. We are now confident in our relationship and understand that we will be able to make it even better. **Maureen & Dino**

I only dipped into this as we are already in a very good relationship however Alisa each chapter has been a little discovery. We understand now why some things work in our relationship and we understand what we should do in order to keep them working. Thank you from the both of us. **Ami & Brett**

Alisa this was easy to read and easy to understand and it was easy to apply. I thought a book on relationships was going to be some kinda rocket science, I was wrong. This is great! Thank you from both of us.
Allen & Maddy

We bought this book not because we felt there was anything wrong in our relationship but because we, well, just needed to make sure we did not do anything too screwy. Alisa the advice you give here was just right on. Mei and I felt absolutely it was written like you knew us personally. It really helped us feel good that we are on the right track. Lance & Mei

Has this book helped your relationship? Have you found it helped you make it better? Did you find a chapter that seemed to have been written just for you? I would love to hear from you. Please use the email address below and let me know how it helped. Do not forget to include your first names and attach a photograph if possible.

info@ultimateguidetotheperfectrelationship.com